in the Classroom

Book I: Activities for autumn through Christmas

by

CHIYO ARAKI

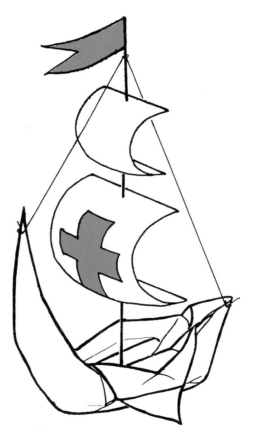

CHARLES E. TUTTLE COMPANY

Rutland, Vermont   Tokyo, Japan

Representatives

For the British Isles & Continental Europe:
SIMON & SCHUSTER INTERNATIONAL GROUP, *London*

For Australasia:
BOOKWISE INTERNATIONAL
1 Jeanes Street, Beverley, 5009, South Australia

Published by the Charles E. Tuttle Company, Inc.
of Rutland, Vermont and Tokyo, Japan
with editorial offices at
Suido 1-chome, 2–6, Bunkyo-ku, Tokyo, Japan

© 1965 by Charles E. Tuttle Co., Inc.

Library of Congress Catalog Card No. 65–13412

International Standard Book No. 0–8048–0452–4

First printing, 1965
Fourteenth printing, 1988

Printed in Japan

Origami in the Classroom

Introduction

My hope is to introduce the unique Japanese origami to American children by adapting it to annual events and holidays in the U.S., as these are always important in the lives of children.

Creativity is born from vision and imagination in our work, making life more enjoyable. Presenting children with tasks they can do by themselves promotes interest and confidence. Children will begin to enjoy art and become capable in it.

Art in the primary school should have much variety. It should provide nourishment for the children's future. Introduce them to many kinds of art to help them develop techniques to which they become accustomed, so that they may taste the joy of expressing themselves in their own way.

This book gives the children coordinated material and makes origami more than something merely to "pass-away-the-time." The pupils may fold, cut, paste, draw, tie, and then use what they have made in their play. Through the use of crayon, pastel, and water-paint they will be practicing the many techniques required in drawing.

By necessity they will become acquainted with geometric figures such as the triangle and the square. Origami requires precision. It is impossible to skip a step. You cannot make the figure unless you fold the paper flat with much care, step by step, along the correct folding lines.

All can enjoy this book, as the steps are explained in detail with pictures beginning with one square sheet of paper. The subjects included were chosen among those used during my ten years with the children of the dependents' school at the American Air Force Base in Yokota, Tokyo. To help your planning, the required time, the necessary material, and the grade level have been noted. However, if sufficient time is given for learning, it is possible to use any figure for all grades. There are, doubtless, many other materials and many other ways to use the finished article than those I have mentioned, so please experiment freely with any new materials or uses which are suitable to the circumstances.

The occasions used in this book are chosen among events from September through December.

With deepest gratitude to my dear friends, Miss Dorothy Bernard, Miss Gloria Paar, and Mr. and Mrs. Ronald G. Korver, for their generous help.

CHIYO ARAKI

Table of Contents

Columbus Day

Ship A

LEVEL: Lower grades

TIME: 50 minutes

MATERIALS: Folding paper (white 7″ × 7″)
Drawing paper (white or blue 12″ × 9″)
Color crayons or water paint
Paste

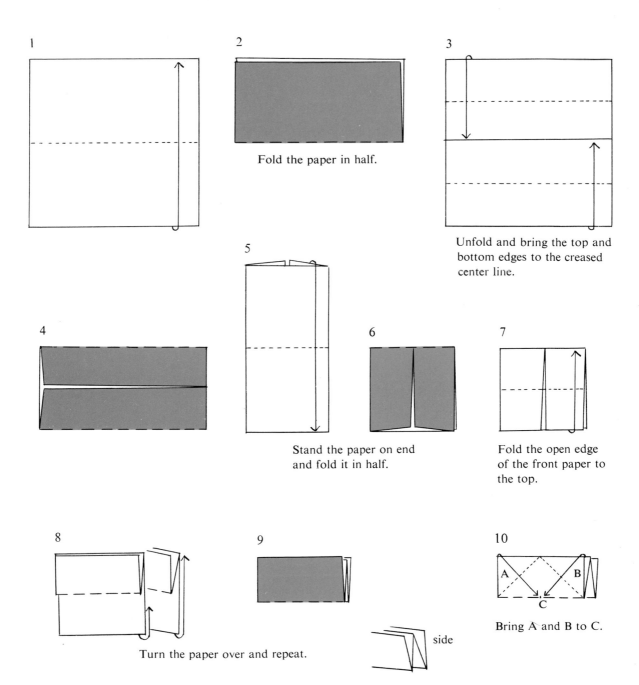

1

2

Fold the paper in half.

3

Unfold and bring the top and bottom edges to the creased center line.

4

5

Stand the paper on end and fold it in half.

6

7

Fold the open edge of the front paper to the top.

8

Turn the paper over and repeat.

9

side

10

Bring A and B to C.

10

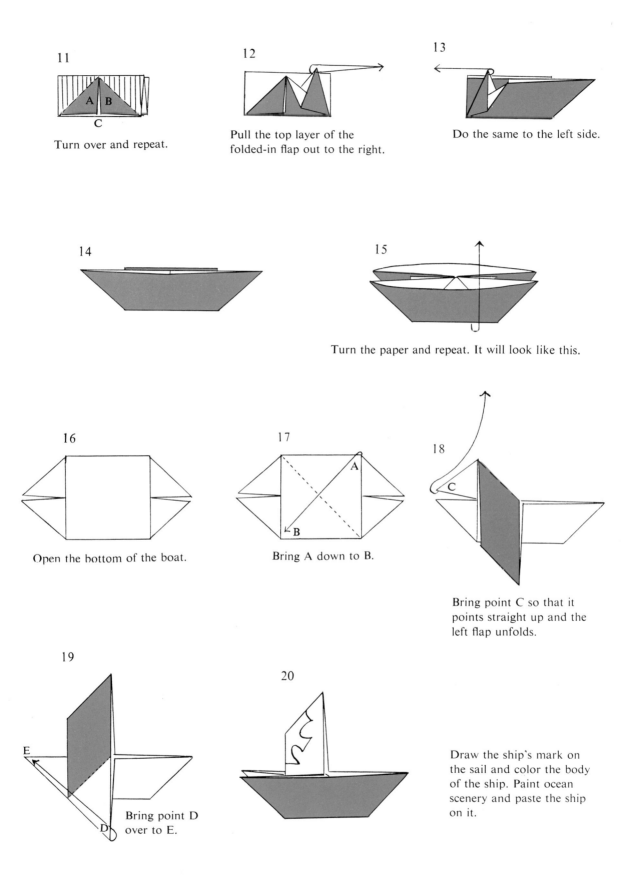

11

Turn over and repeat.

12

Pull the top layer of the folded-in flap out to the right.

13

Do the same to the left side.

14

15

Turn the paper and repeat. It will look like this.

16

Open the bottom of the boat.

17

Bring A down to B.

18

Bring point C so that it points straight up and the left flap unfolds.

19

Bring point D over to E.

20

Draw the ship's mark on the sail and color the body of the ship. Paint ocean scenery and paste the ship on it.

Ship B

LEVEL: Middle grades

TIME: 1 hour

MATERIALS: Folding paper (white 7″×7″)
Drawing paper (white or blue 12″×9″)
Color crayons or water paint
Scissors and paste

Follow figures 1–3 for ship A, page 10.

5

6

7

4

Bring the top and bottom
edges to the center line.

Stand the paper on end
and fold in half.

A   B

C   D

Unfold and bring
the CD edge up
to the AB line.

8

9

10

11

C   D

C   D

O

A

B

Bring C and D, which you folded, down to point O.

Pull the top layer of the folded-
in flap B out to the right. Repeat
with flap A.

12

13

14

Cut left and right above the hull along the front, cutting only a
single layer of paper.

Draw the sails, masts, and flags.
Cut out as necessary. Paint the
ocean scenery and paste the ship
on it.

12

Ship C

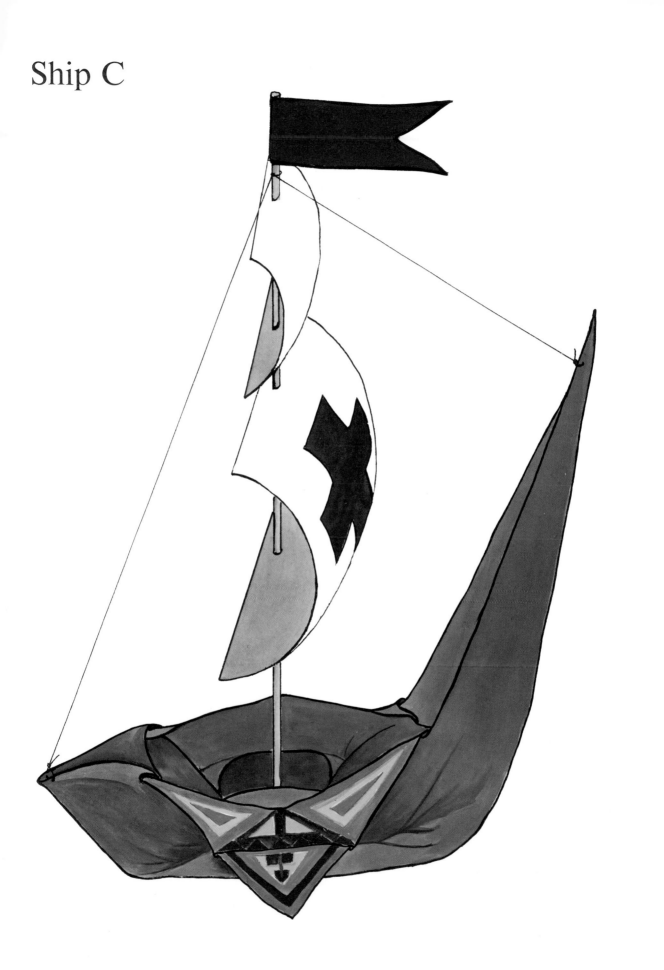

Ship C

MATERIALS: Folding paper (strong brown wrapping paper 15″×15″)
Thin red or white paper for flag
White paper for sails
Bamboo stick or branch for mast
Thread, hole puncher, crayons, and plastic clay (1″×1″×1″) or
potato to hold mast

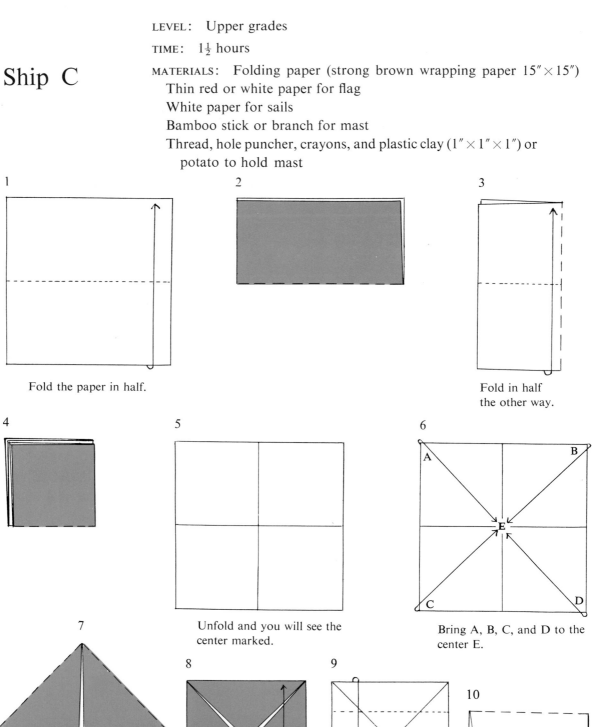

1

Fold the paper in half.

2

3

Fold in half
the other way.

4

5

Unfold and you will see the
center marked.

6

Bring A, B, C, and D to the
center E.

7

8

Fold in half and then
open this last fold.

9

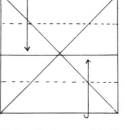

Bring the top and bottom
edges to the creased line
in the center.

10

11

Stand the paper on end and fold in half.

12

Fold the front paper to the top.

13

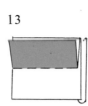

Turn over and repeat.

14

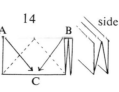

Bring A and B to C.

15

Turn over and repeat.

16

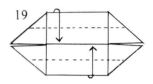

Pull the top layer of the folded-in flap out to the right.

17

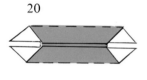

Do the same to the left flap.

18

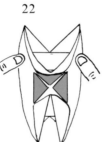

Turn over and repeat. It will look like this.

19

Open the bottom of the boat. Fold the sides in toward the creased line in the center.

20

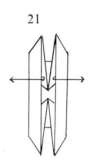

21

Turn the paper over.

22

Open the outside edges and hold them down with your fingers.

23

Open the connecting strip of paper.

24

Press A back and press the boat flat.

25

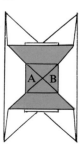

Turn it upside-down and again open the outside edges.

26

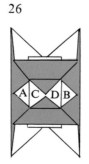

Lift flap B so that D is exposed.

27

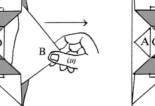

Hold D tightly and pull B.

28

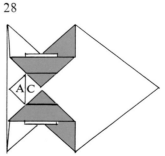

29

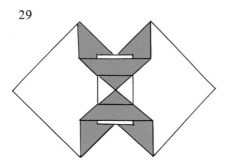

Repeat with side A so that it looks like this.

30

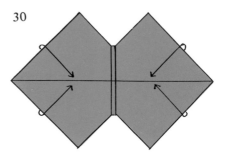

Turn over and bring the four edges to
the creased line in the center.

31

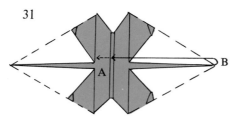

Bring point B under fold A.

32

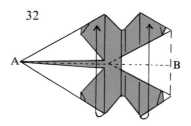

Fold in half along line.

33

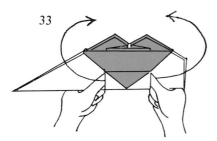

Hold by the small rectangle and put your thumbs
inside the rectangle. Put your next two fingers in
the rectangle on the other side and grasp tightly.
Completely pull out only the folded-in part, with the
back of your hands turning in towards the rectangle,
slowly and carefully.

34

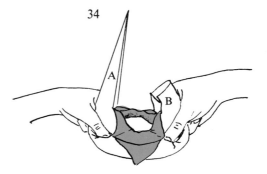

Straighten out A and B.

35

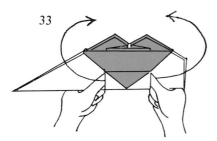

You can see the long seats stick out in the center, and
the bottom should be flat so that the ship stands by itself.

There are many ways to make the mast so devise your own.
Several ways to make the mast holder:
Use clay (plastic) or potatoes.
Make a cardboard box and fill it with plaster of Paris or cement.

16

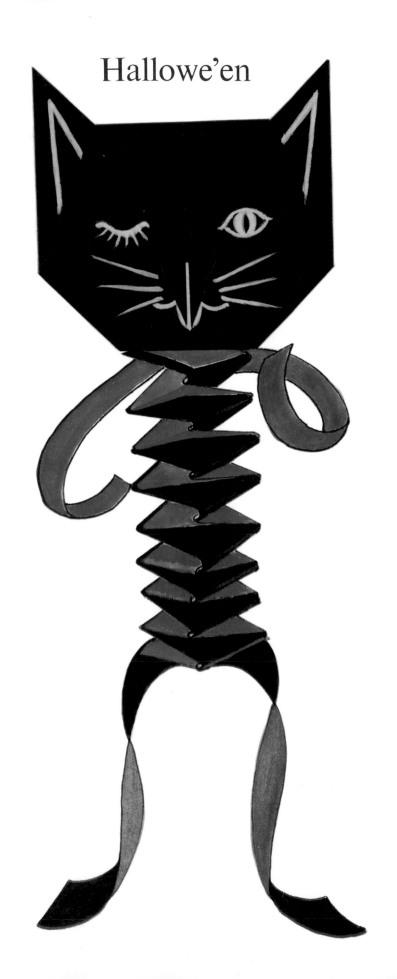

Hallowe'en

LEVEL: Middle grades

TIME: 1½ hours

MATERIALS: Folding paper (black 6″×6″) for face
Construction paper:
    Orange (18″×1″) for body
    Black (18″×1″) for body
    Orange (4½″×½″) two pieces for arms
    Black (9″×1″) for legs

Pussy Cat

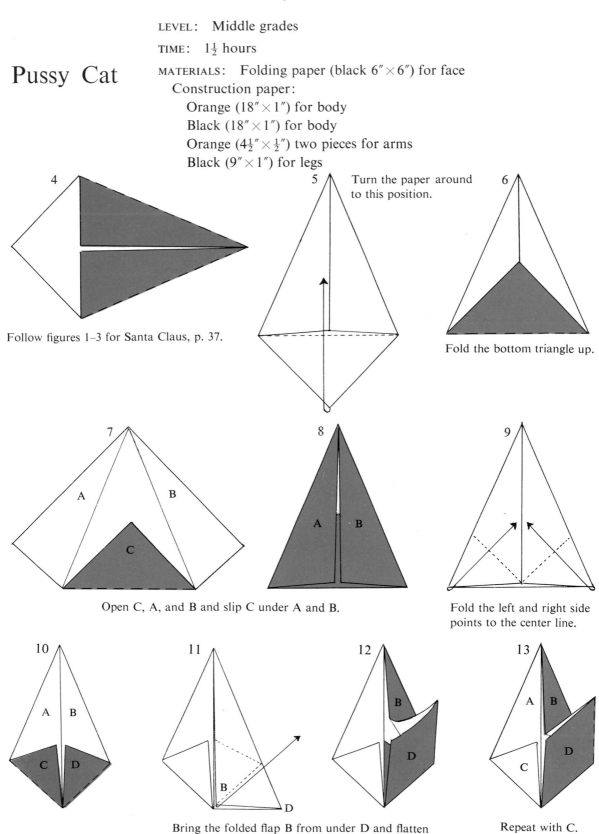

4

Follow figures 1–3 for Santa Claus, p. 37.

5 Turn the paper around to this position.

6 Fold the bottom triangle up.

7 Open C, A, and B and slip C under A and B.

8

9 Fold the left and right side points to the center line.

10

11 Bring the folded flap B from under D and flatten it to form a diamond shape.

12

13 Repeat with C.

18

14

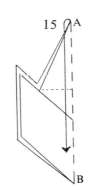

15

A

B

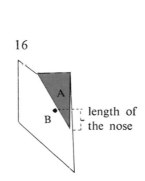

16

length of the nose

B A

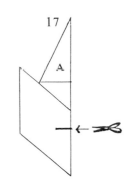

17

A

Turn over and fold the paper in half along the straight line AB.

Bring point A down. For the length of the nose, mark point B by the edge of triangle A.

Open A and draw a horizontal line from the mark to the right edge and then cut along this line.

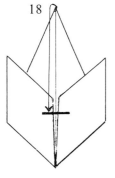

18

19

20

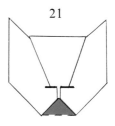

21

Unfold the center fold and slip the top point through the opening.

Fold up a little of the bottom point.

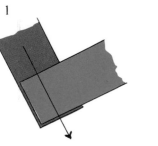

22

side

Turn the paper over and stand the nose up. Make the eyes, mouth, whiskers, and tongue with scraps of colored construction paper.

23

BODY
1. Paste the end of orange paper across the end of the black paper.
2. Bring the black paper over the orange. Do not leave space between the orange and black.
3. Bring the orange over the black. Repeat this to the end of the paper and paste the ends. Paste the head onto the body. Paste the arms under the neck and paste the legs to bottom.

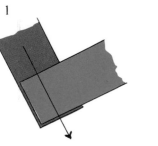

1

2

3

Bat

Bat

LEVEL: Lower grades

TIME: 45 minutes

MATERIALS: Folding paper (black 6″ × 6″)
Construction paper (12″ × 9″) for drawing scenery
Crayons or water paint, scissors, and paste

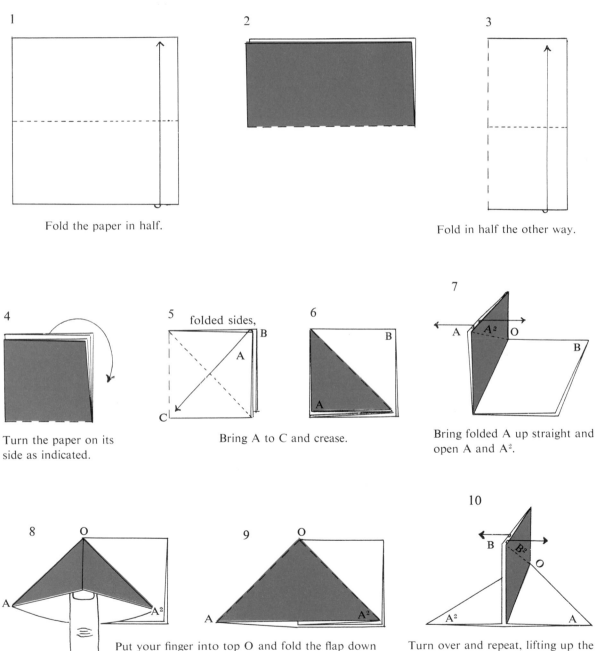

1

Fold the paper in half.

2

3

Fold in half the other way.

4

Turn the paper on its side as indicated.

5 folded sides,

Bring A to C and crease.

6

7

Bring folded A up straight and open A and A².

8

9

Put your finger into top O and fold the flap down to form a triangle with O, A, and A².

10

Turn over and repeat, lifting up the square corner and then opening it.

21

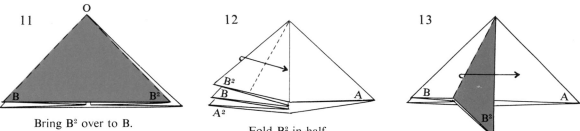

11   Bring B² over to B.

12   Fold B² in half.

13   Bring folded B² over to A.

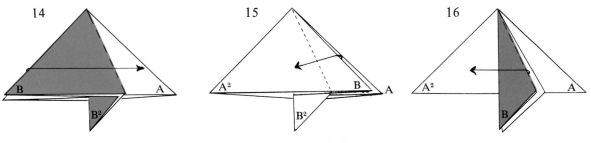

14

15   Repeat with side B.

16

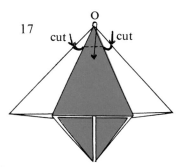

17   Cut along the lines for ears and fold point O down to the front.

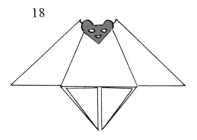

18   Make the eyes and mouth.

Cat

LEVEL: Lower grades

TIME: 45 minutes

MATERIALS: Folding paper (6″ × 6″) two pieces
Construction paper (12″ × 9″)
Crayons or water paint, paste, and scissors

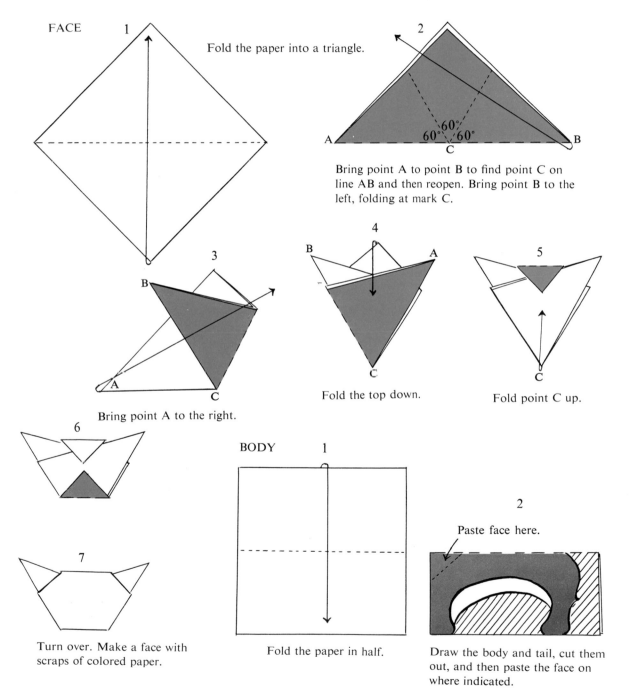

FACE

1 Fold the paper into a triangle.

2 Bring point A to point B to find point C on line AB and then reopen. Bring point B to the left, folding at mark C.

3 Bring point A to the right.

4 Fold the top down.

5 Fold point C up.

6 —

7 Turn over. Make a face with scraps of colored paper.

BODY

1 Fold the paper in half.

2 Paste face here.

Draw the body and tail, cut them out, and then paste the face on where indicated.

23

Cat on a Jack o'Lantern

Jack o'Lantern

Construction paper:
   Green   (5″ × ¼″ or ½″) 4 pieces for arms and legs
            (6″ × 5″) for hat
   Orange   (2″ × 2″) for hands and feet
Thread of any color (7″), toothpick, bamboo stick or branch

1

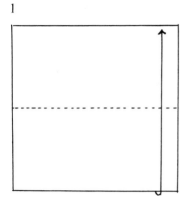

Fold the paper in half.

2

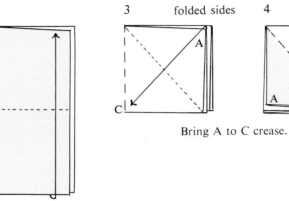

Fold in half again.

3   folded sides

4

Bring A to C crease.

5

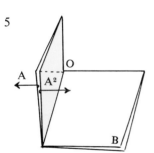

Hold A up straight and
open A and A².

6

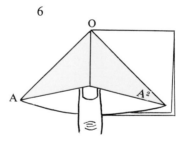

Put your finger inside to top O and press
the flap down to form triangle O, A, A².

7

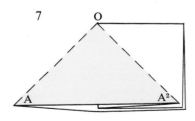

8

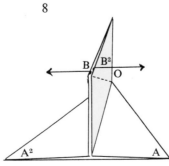

Turn over and repeat.

9

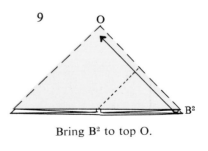

Bring B² to top O.

25

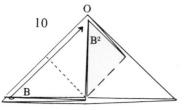

10

O

B²

B

Repeat with side B.

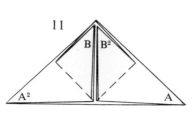

11

B B²

A²

A

Turn over and repeat with A and A².

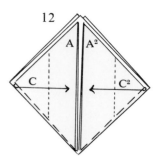

12

A A²

C C²

Turn the paper around and bring C and C² to the center line.

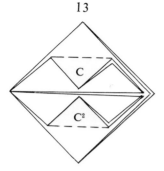

13

C

C²

Turn over and repeat.

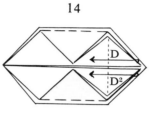

14

D

D²

Fold triangles D and D² to the left.

15

C² C

D D²

Fold D and D² over into C and C² triangles' pockets.

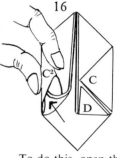

16

C²

C

D

To do this, open the triangle pockets with fingers and slip the edge in.

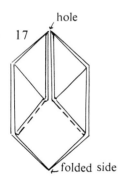

hole

17

folded side

Turn over and repeat on the same end.

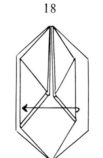

18

Close the right side to the left so that the plain side is showing.

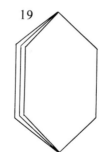

19

Turn over and repeat.

hole

20

Draw the face between the dotted lines indicated.

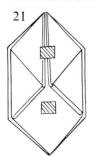

21

Paste the arms and legs on both sides at the places marked. Blow through the hole carefully.

5″

$\frac{1}{4}″$ or $\frac{1}{2}″$

ARMS AND LEGS

HANDS AND FEET

For arms and legs, take four pieces of paper and make accordion folds. To make hands, fold orange paper (2″ square) two times. Draw one hand on the top and cut out all at one time.

26

Jack o'Lantern

LEAF

HANGING

Tie one end of the thread to a toothpick.
Pull the other end of the thread through
a hole in a leaf.
Tie the thread to a bamboo stick very
tightly.
Slip the toothpick into the hole in the tip
of the Jack o'Lantern.

Basket A

LEVEL: Upper grades

TIME: 30 minutes

MATERIALS: Folding paper (6″×6″, or desired size)

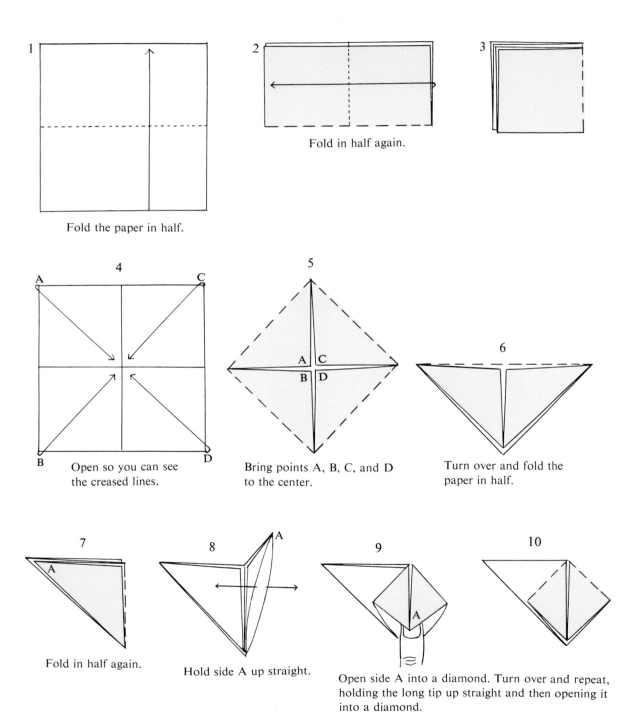

1 Fold the paper in half.

2 Fold in half again.

3

4 Open so you can see the creased lines.

5 Bring points A, B, C, and D to the center.

6 Turn over and fold the paper in half.

7 Fold in half again.

8 Hold side A up straight.

9 Open side A into a diamond. Turn over and repeat, holding the long tip up straight and then opening it into a diamond.

10

28

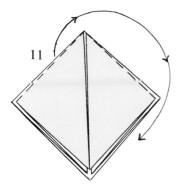

11

Turn the paper upside-down.

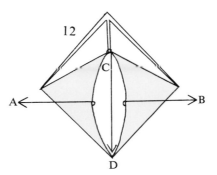

12

Open the front paper A and B
to the left and right. Bring down
point C to D.

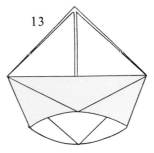

13

Press down into a rectangle.

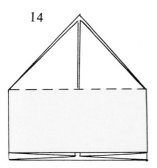

14

Turn it over and repeat.

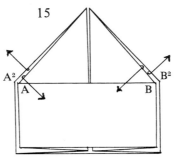

15

Open sides A and A², B and B².

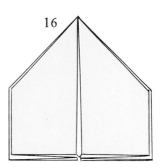

16

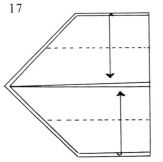

17

Turn the paper on its side.

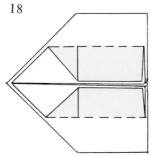

18

Bring both edges to
the center line.

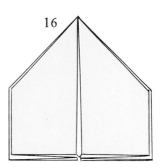

19

Bring C to the right.

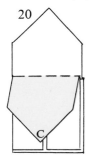

20

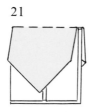

21

Turn over and repeat.

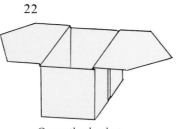

22

Open the basket.

Party Baskets

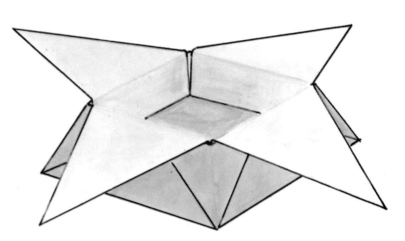

Basket B

LEVEL: All grades

TIME: 20–40 minutes

MATERIALS: Folding paper (6″×6″ or desired size)

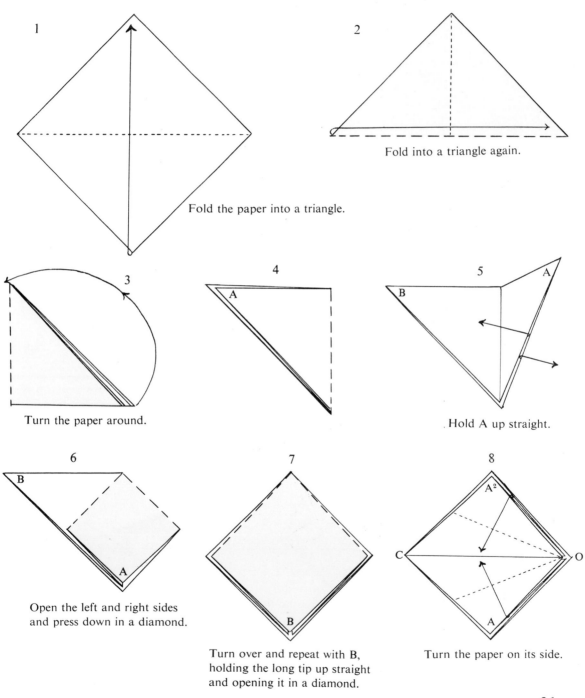

1

Fold the paper into a triangle.

2

Fold into a triangle again.

3

Turn the paper around.

4

5

Hold A up straight.

6

Open the left and right sides
and press down in a diamond.

7

Turn over and repeat with B,
holding the long tip up straight
and opening it in a diamond.

8

Turn the paper on its side.

31

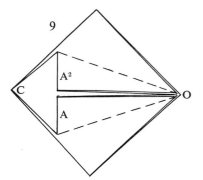

9

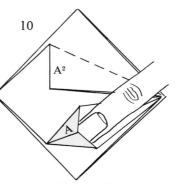

10

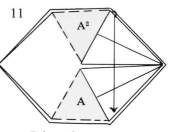

11

Bring A^2 over to A.

Bring A and A^2 to CO line so it looks like this.

Open A with your finger and press it down. Repeat with A^2.

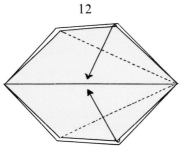

12

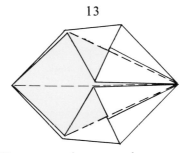

13

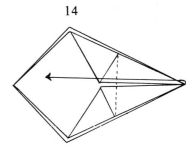

14

Turn over and repeat.

You can see three creased lines. Bring both sides to the center crease. Turn over and repeat.

Bring one of the points all the way to the left. Turn over and repeat.

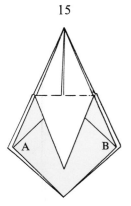

15

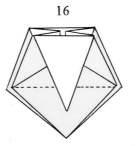

16

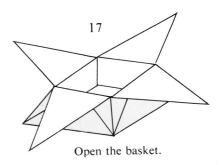

17

Open the basket.

Bring the top flap A to the opposite side B and fold down the point.

Turn over and repeat so that it looks like this.
The dotted line indicated is to be the bottom.

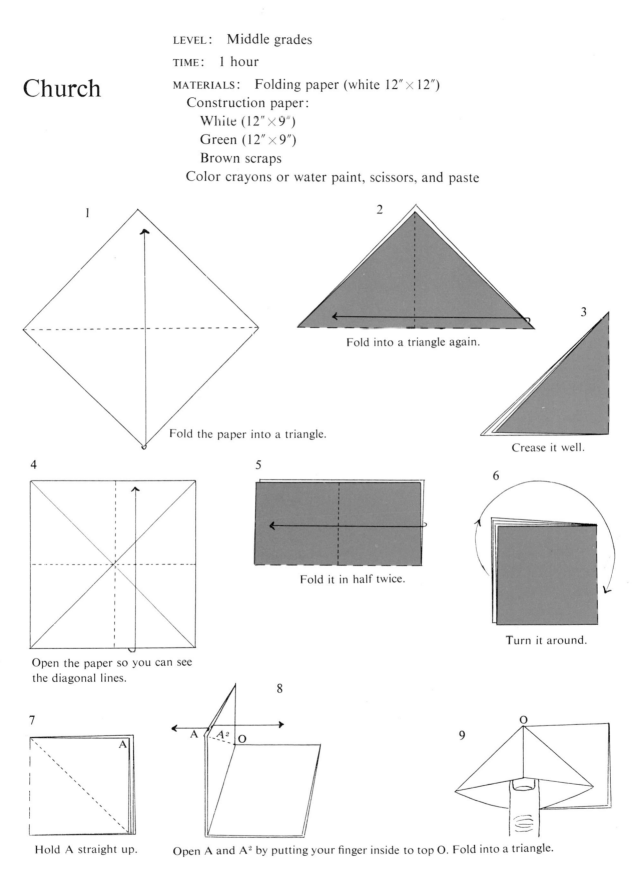

Church

LEVEL: Middle grades

TIME: 1 hour

MATERIALS: Folding paper (white 12″ × 12″)
Construction paper:
White (12″ × 9″)
Green (12″ × 9″)
Brown scraps
Color crayons or water paint, scissors, and paste

1

Fold the paper into a triangle.

2

Fold into a triangle again.

3

Crease it well.

4

Open the paper so you can see the diagonal lines.

5

Fold it in half twice.

6

Turn it around.

7

Hold A straight up.

8

Open A and A² by putting your finger inside to top O. Fold into a triangle.

9

33

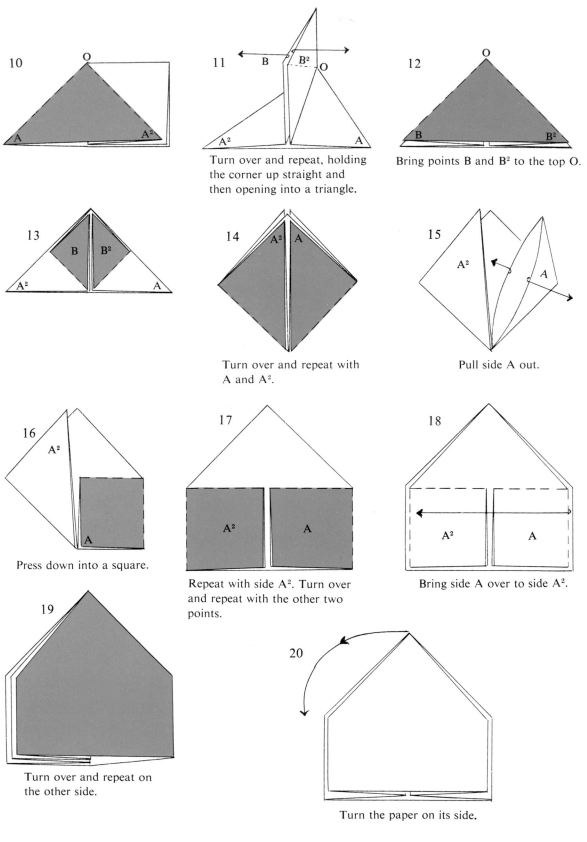

10

11 Turn over and repeat, holding the corner up straight and then opening into a triangle.

12 Bring points B and B² to the top O.

13

14 Turn over and repeat with A and A².

15 Pull side A out.

16 Press down into a square.

17 Repeat with side A². Turn over and repeat with the other two points.

18 Bring side A over to side A².

19 Turn over and repeat on the other side.

20 Turn the paper on its side.

34

Church at Christmas

pupil's name

21

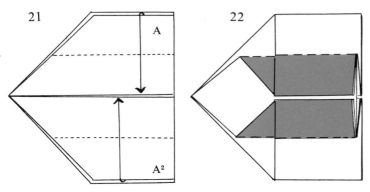

Bring sides A and A² to the creased line in the center. Turn over and repeat on the other side.

22

23

Turn the paper around.

24

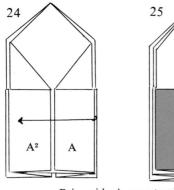

Bring side A over to side A².

25

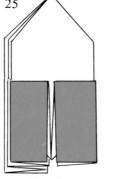

26

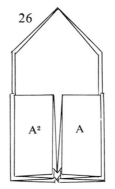

Turn over and repeat.

27

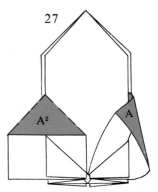

Open side A² and press it down flat to form the roof shape. Repeat with side A.

28

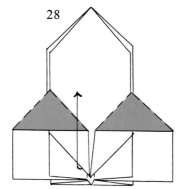

Bring the triangle which points to the center of the bottom up and fold it back.

29

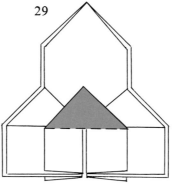

Turn over and repeat. Draw the doors, windows, and bell. Cut a cross and paste it on the top.

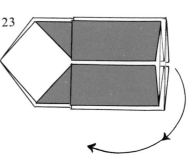

TREE

Cut out two trees. Slit one halfway down. Slit the other halfway up.

Fit the two trees together.

*The church stands up by itself, so if you make two Christmas trees with green construction paper that stand and use them on either side of the church, it will look more attractive.

LEVEL: Lower grades

TIME: 1 hour

Santa Claus

MATERIALS: Folding paper (red 6″×6″) two pieces
Construction paper:
White (two circles, one 7″ and the other 1½″ in diameter)
Blue (12″×9″)
Green, red, and yellow scraps

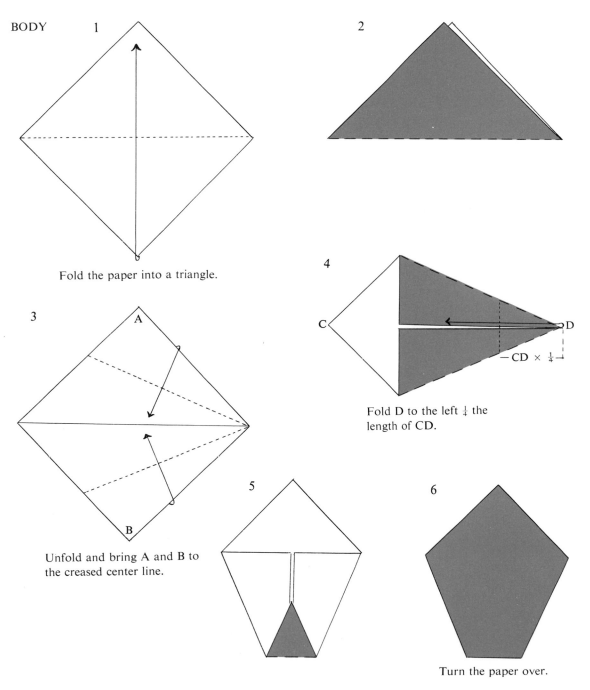

BODY

1 Fold the paper into a triangle.

2

3 Unfold and bring A and B to the creased center line.

4 Fold D to the left ¼ the length of CD.

$-CD \times \frac{1}{4}-$

5

6 Turn the paper over.

37

Santa Claus

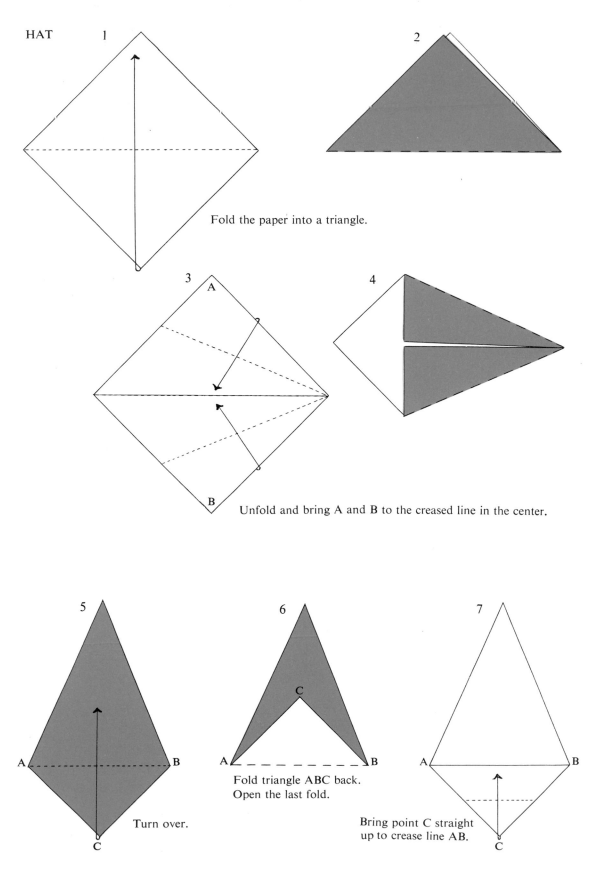

HAT

1. Fold the paper into a triangle.

2.

3. Unfold and bring A and B to the creased line in the center.

4.

5. Turn over.

6. Fold triangle ABC back.
Open the last fold.

7. Bring point C straight up to crease line AB.

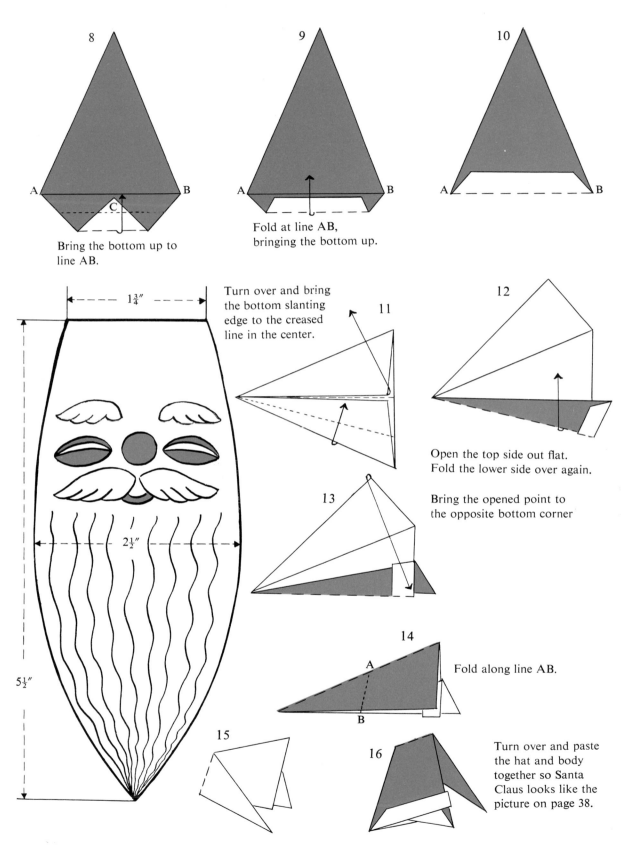

8

A   C   B

Bring the bottom up to
line AB.

9

A   B

Fold at line AB,
bringing the bottom up.

10

A   B

Turn over and bring
the bottom slanting
edge to the creased
line in the center.

11

12

Open the top side out flat.
Fold the lower side over again.

Bring the opened point to
the opposite bottom corner

13

14

A

B

Fold along line AB.

15

16

Turn over and paste
the hat and body
together so Santa
Claus looks like the
picture on page 38.

1¾″

2½″

5½″

40